GW00320096

Assert yourself

How to find your voice and make your mark

THE SIMPLE APPROACH SERIES
from Everywoman Ltd
www.everywoman.co.uk

© Everywoman Ltd 2006   Welcome and 'Words of Wisdom'
sections.
All other text © Bloomsbury Publishing Plc 2004
A & C Black Publishers Ltd 2006

First published in 2004 by
Bloomsbury Publishing Plc
38 Soho Square
London W1D 3HB

This edition published by
Everywoman Ltd
12 Hurlingham Business Park
Sulivan Road, London SW6 3DU

British Library Cataloguing in Publication Data
A CIP record for this book is available from the British Library.

ISBN 10: 0–9552782–0–1
ISBN 13: 978–0–9552782–0–4

Design by Fiona Pike, Pike Design, Winchester
Typeset by RefineCatch Limited, Bungay, Suffolk
Printed in Italy by Legoprint

Contents

Welcome to everywoman

The leading authority

everywoman is recognised as the leading authority and provider of services to enhance the status of women in the UK economy. Our unique insight into the challenges women face has led us to design an exciting range of tools to overcome any hurdles and motivate women to engineer their own personal development and business growth.

Working in partnership with large corporations and government who support the work we do, we *know* what women need to achieve. Our authority has been endorsed by many flourishing women business leaders who regularly contribute to our one-day conferences and participate in our awards programme. In this series of books, too, their involvement is harnessed through our **expert panel** which brings together an exclusive group of successful women whose 'words of wisdom' offer you precious inspiration and motivation – unique to **everywoman**.

The **everywoman** commitment to support women in business acknowledges that a woman's career journey may take many routes. You may be running your own business or in employment but the priorities and values you hold remain the same: success at work, financial independence, and a personal and family wellbeing. That's why we're proud today to support all women who seek to develop their lives through work.

everywoman model for business success

We firmly believe that the foundation stone of any successful business revolves around three key principles:

- **Learning**
  Keeping up-to-date with the latest thinking, technology and leadership skills is vital for any woman in business. To face up to growing challenges, we have to be creative, innovative and prepared to risk a new idea on an old problem.
- **Networking**
  Whether you're working independently or as part of a busy office, building new business contacts through online and offline networking will help you establish and grow your customer base and create a network of positive referrals.
- **Inspiration**
  Role models are an essential part of life. We all want to be motivated and often need to find new energy sources to face our fears and leap into the business unknown.

What everywoman can do for *you*

When you become a member of **everywoman**, you are joining successful women who value shared ideas and mutual support. **Free** membership gives:

- up-to-the minute business news to keep you bang up-to-date with the latest business thinking
- exclusive access to our online bulletin boards for you to build your own business support network
- regular newsletters delivered to your in-box to inform and inspire – and offer you exclusive priority notice of **everywoman** events and special offers

Who makes up the everywoman community?

The **everywoman** community covers a wide diversity of professions and services. You'll engage with recruitment agencies, manufacturers, childcare managers, industrialists, fashion designers, and many others. They all have the power to connect you with others, and offer advice and reassurance.

everywoman goes live

Although you will meet **everywoman** members online, you can be introduced face-to-face at our events:

- **Grow your business conferences**
  One-day conferences throughout the UK combining interactive workshops, motivational speakers, and inspirational advice from leading women entrepreneurs.
- **Personal and Business Mastery seminars**
  Designed for top-flight women in business, these dynamic seminars develop your innate leadership qualities and refine your interpersonal skills.
- **Business Fundamentals workshops**
  Practical half-day workshops delivered by experienced practitioners.
- **The Inspirational Female Leader**© A programme to enable organisations to develop the leadership potential of their female employees.

When you're back in the office

Day-to-day, we know how valuable it is for you to keep in touch with the support and business advice you get from an **everywoman** event. That's why we created this **Simple Approach** series: books jam-packed with practical tips, anecdotes, and 'words of wisdom' from leading women in business. Whatever your situation, whether you're running your own business or working in a corporate organisation, you'll find information here to help you.

A word from the sponsor

IBM is delighted that, as a founding sponsor, our continuing relationship with **everywoman** allows us to sponsor this important series of books.

As a global technology and services business, IBM is committed to championing women in business and views **everywoman** as a key player in the effort to raise the profile of women, who more than ever are driving the economy.

As women play an ever greater part in the growth of the economies of the UK and Europe, they are increasingly recognising the importance of learning in the financial and management spheres of business. IBM espouses that one of the most effective aids to learning is mentoring, in either a formal way or in an informal fashion such as having access to women who have walked the same path in business and can offer their words of wisdom. We believe this series of books is a key partner to the mentoring and learning process.

The **everywoman Simple Approach** series covers the core skills that are vital for any business to prosper in today's world. IBM recognises the need of entrepreneurs and women in business to develop the skills, learn the values and assess the priorities discussed in this series, while also demonstrating how you can still achieve real flexibility and work-life balance. We believe this series of books will be an invaluable tool in assisting you on your journey to successfully strengthening your business.

Women in the UK economy

In the UK, a country where only 1 in 10 working men has a female boss, women still make a substantial contribution to the economy. Businesses in women-majority ownership contribute approximately £130 billion turnover to the UK economy (Source: Meg Munn MP, Deputy Minister for Women, Nov 2005)

- Nearly 7% of women are owners/managers of their own business compared with 15.8% of men (GEM: Global Entrepreneurship Monitor January 2004)
- Women are half as likely to start-up in business as men: 3.1% of the female adult population start up a business independently compared with 6% of men (GEM January 2004)
- Less than 30% of self-employed people in the UK are women (Small Business Service 'A Strategic Framework for Women's Enterprise', 2003)

'Pink' potential, however, still has far to go. There would be 0.75 million more businesses in the UK if we could reach the same level of female entrepreneurship as exists in the US (Gordon Brown, Chancellor of the Exchequer, Advancing Enterprise Conference, 2005). Which is one important reason why we set up the **everywoman** Awards programme.

Showcasing women's business brilliance

The **everywoman** annual Awards programme is dedicated to showcasing the achievements of women who have started their own business often in the most difficult and adverse circumstances.

With serial international entrepreneur Lady Lynn Forester de Rothschild as Patron, these Awards create a stage on which inspirational stories play a significant role in encouraging other women to take those first nervous steps into enterprise. We're proud of the powerful role models our Awards finalists and winners create.

For more information on this year's programme, go to **www.everywoman.co.uk/awards**.

Karen Gill & Maxine Benson
Co-founders, Everywoman Ltd

everywoman expert panel

In our **Simple Approach** series, these 12 women overleaf – and more – have been exclusively selected for their expertise to give you access to real-life role models and offer their 'words of wisdom' to inspire and encourage you. A full list of contributing experts throughout the series can be found at **www.everywoman.co.uk/simpleapproach**.

Deirdre Bounds, i-to-i.com

Deirdre launched i-to-i from a Leeds bedsit. Now an international organisation with offices in the UK, US, Ireland, and Australia, and 130 staff worldwide, i-to-i sends 4,000 people a year to support 500 worthwhile projects in 27 countries. It also trains 10,000 people as TEFL teachers.

Dawn Gibbins MBE DBA (Hons), Flowcrete Group plc

Dawn started Flowcrete in 1982 with her father. Now as a leading manufacturer of specialist flooring and a £32m turnover, it has 26 offices and 8 manufacturing centres globally. Rewarded with the Veuve Clicquot Business Woman of the Year, Dawn also accepted an MBE in 1994.

Emma Harrison, A4e Ltd

Emma was left in charge of her father's small training company, when he moved to Germany. By the first year, she'd earned £1 million turnover and in 1991 founded A4e Ltd to deliver social change on behalf of the government. Now employing 1500 staff, Emma starred in C4's 'Making a Million'.

Sharon Hilditch, Crystal Clear International

Having started in business with her first beauty salon, Sharon formed Crystal Clear International in 1995, with a £15,000 bank loan. It is now one of the leading anti-aging skin care brands in the international beauty market and was winner of the NatWest Everywoman Award in 2004.

Liz Jackson, Great Guns Marketing

With no advanced education, Liz launched her telemarketing company with the help of The Prince's Trust's £1,000 grant and a £4,000 loan. Today, with more than £2m turnover, it has 9 regional branches across UK and Ireland. This is an amazing achievement, as Liz is totally blind and only in her early 30s.

Stephanie Manuel, Stagecoach Theatre Arts plc

With a passion for theatre, Stephanie started Stagecoach in 1988 with business partner David Sprigg, and franchising began in 1994. With more than 560 Stagecoach schools in the UK, the business now extends to three continents, with 30 overseas schools.

Joy Nichols, Nichols Employment Agency

Joy started her first business in 1979 as a freelance secretary before officially establishing The Nichols Agency in 1984 which is now one of the most successfully black-owned businesses in London. With a satellite office in Luton, they focus on the health and social care sector.

Avril Owton, The Cloud Hotel

A former dancer, Avril now owns the award-winning Cloud Hotel in Brockenhurst. Having overcome enormous challenges, she was voted Hampshire Business Woman of the Year, and is a recognised motivator for female peers and regular speaker for national organisations.

Sally Preston, Babylicious

With a food retail and manufacturing background, Sally set up Babylicious in 2001, producing frozen baby food. She re-mortgaged her home and borrowed from her parents to set up from her kitchen and dining room. Her success has been recognised by many awards (including the HSBC 'Start up Stars' Award, for 'Best New Business').

Laura Tenison MBE, JoJo Maman Bébé

Laura launched JoJo Maman Bébé 13 years ago, growing from a start-up to over 140 employees and a turnover of around £11m, without any bank loan or outside investor. Welsh Entrepreneur of the Year 2003 and Harpers & Queen Entrepreneur of the year 2005, Laura received an MBE in 2004.

Christina Vaughan, Image Source

Founded in 1999, Image Source is the world's leading independent producer and brand for creative and commercial royalty free stock photography. With more than 50 employees based in London, Cologne and New York, the company won the Queen's Award for Enterprise in 2005.

Perween Warsi CBE, S & A Foods

Perween began her business making ethnic finger foods from her kitchen and in 1986, founded S & A Foods, winning her first major contract to supply chilled and frozen dishes to Asda and Safeway. In 2002, Perween received the CBE for services to business.

How assertive are you?

Answer the questions and work out where you are on the assertiveness scale, then read the guidance points for ideas on how to get the most positive response from those around you.

How often do you feel 'put upon' at work?

a) Regularly, but it is what I expect.

b) I generally feel in control of my workload.

c) Colleagues have finally realised that I am not to be imposed upon.

How do you feel when someone seeks your opinion?

a) Very grateful as it happens so rarely.

b) I feel happy that they value my judgments.

c) Colleagues usually know my opinions already—if they have to ask they weren't listening!

You're having a discussion with someone who isn't giving you a chance to respond. What do you do?

a) Wait and listen. They may have something valuable to say.

b) Make eye contact and let my body language show I'm about to speak, before starting to make my point.

c) Talk louder than them—they'll soon stop and listen!

If a colleague asks you to do something which you feel isn't your responsibility, what do you do?
a) Try to fit it in—it's important to be as helpful as possible.
b) It may provide a useful learning experience, so try to fit it in, but make sure they know I'm doing them a favour.
c) Refuse—it's their job and their responsibility.

How do you feel about other members of your team?
a) I worry that they don't think much of me.
b) I respect their experience. We're all on the same team.
c) I don't think much of them, so try to avoid them so I can get on with my job.

A colleague stops by to chat but stays too long, preventing you from getting on with your work. What do you do?
a) Let them stay, and resign myself to staying late to finish.
b) Explain that I have a deadline to meet and suggest they return another time.
c) Tell them to stop bothering me—can't they see I'm busy?

You suspect a colleague dislikes you, but aren't sure why. How do you deal with this?
a) Pretend I'm unaware of their attitude and try my best to avoid them.
b) Talk to them to find out the reason for their aversion.
c) Be confrontational in my dealings with them so that next time they will think twice about being haughty.

a = **1**, **b** = **2**, and **c** = **3**. Now add up your scores.

Chapter **1** is useful to everyone as it suggests different ways of projecting a more positive image, including paying attention to body language and reacting differently to different character types.

- **5–10:** You're at the passive end of the assertiveness scale, and if you're not careful you'll end up being taken for granted which will make you very unhappy. Assertiveness is not simply about talking more and louder; read chapter **2** to discover new ways of developing presence—let people know you are there! Learn how to control others' perceptions of you by reading chapter **5**. Bullying is never acceptable. If you think you're being treated unfairly or being bullied, chapter **6** offers advice on dealing with your situation.

- **11–15:** You have a balanced, assertive approach to your work and colleagues, which would be good to build upon. Develop your non-verbal communication and leadership skills (chapters **5** and **7**) in order to hone your abilities and achieve your full potential.

- **16–21:** You're in danger of being aggressive and making enemies. Perhaps your behaviour stems from a lack of confidence in your abilities, and you're overcompensating for this. Chapters **3** and **7** offer ideas for building confidence. Remember to communicate effectively by listening actively and mirroring your colleagues' body language (chapters **2** and **4**). You're all working for the same side, so you don't feel the need to compete for supremacy!

Communicating assertively at work

Do you find that people get the better of you, that you're not given the respect you deserve, or that you're always the one who draws the short straw and ends up doing things that you would rather not do? Does this end up making you resentful or unhappy because you feel helpless and unable to confront the situation?

Assertiveness is an approach to communication that honours your choices as well as those of the person you are communicating with. It's not about being aggressive and steamrollering others into submission. Rather, it's about seeking and exchanging opinions, developing a full understanding of the issues, and negotiating a win-win situation.

Ask yourself these questions to determine your level of assertiveness:

- Do you feel 'put upon' or ignored in your exchanges with others?
- Are you unable to speak your mind and ask for what you want?
- Do you find it difficult to stand up for yourself in a discussion?

■ **Are you inordinately grateful when someone seeks your opinion and takes it into account?**

If you answer 'yes' to most of these questions, you may need to consider becoming more assertive.

Step one: Choose the right approach

Becoming assertive is all about making choices that meet your needs and the needs of the situation. Sometimes it's appropriate to be passive. If you were facing a snarling dog, you might not want to provoke an attack by looking for a win-win situation! There may be other occasions when aggression is the answer. However, this is still assertive behaviour as *you*, rather than other people or situations, are in control of how you react.

TOP TIP

After a lifetime of being the way they are, some people are daunted by the prospect of change. But if you don't change what you do, you'll never change what you get. All it takes to change is a decision. Once you have made that decision, you will naturally observe yourself in situations, notice what you do and don't do well, and then you can try out new behaviours to see what works for you.

✔ You may find it helpful to investigate some specially tailored training courses so that you can try out some approaches before taking on a colleague or manager in a 'live' situation. Assertiveness does not develop overnight: it takes time, practice, and patience.

Step two: Practise projecting a positive image

✔ Use 'winning' language. Rather than saying 'I always come off worst!' say 'I've learned a great deal from doing lots of different things in my career. I'm now ready to move on'. Replacing negative statements with positive affirmations is a simple yet powerful way of taking control in your life.

✔ Visualise yourself how you would like to be. Form a mental image of an assertive you, and then make the image as real as possible, and feel the sensation of being in control. Perhaps there have been moments in your life when you naturally felt like this, a time when you have excelled.

Recapture that moment and 'live' it again. Imagine how it would be if you felt like that in other areas of your life. Determine to make this your goal and recall this powerful image or feeling when you are getting disheartened. It will re-energise you and keep you on track.

TOP TIP
If you are small in stature, it's easy to think
you can't have presence because people
will overlook you. But many of the
most successful people in business
and in entertainment are physically
quite small. Adopting an assertive
communication style and body
language has the effect of making
you look more imposing. Assume
you have impact, visualise it,
feel it, breathe it.

Step three: Condition others to take you seriously

This can be done through non-verbal as well as verbal communication.

✔ If someone is talking over you and you're finding it difficult to get a word in edgeways, you can hold up your hand signalling 'stop' as you begin to speak. 'I hear what you are saying but I would like to put forward an alternative viewpoint . . . '

✔ Always take responsibility for your communication. Use the 'I' word. 'I would like . . . ', 'I don't agree . . . ', 'I am uncomfortable with this . . . '

✔ Being aware of non-verbal communication signals can also help you build rapport. If you mirror what others are doing when they are communicating with you, it will help you get a sense of where they are coming from and how to respond in the most helpful way.

TOP TIP
Until you get used to being assertive, you may find it hard to say 'no' to people. One useful technique is to say, 'I'd like to think about this first. I'll get back to you shortly.' Giving yourself time and space to rehearse your response can be really helpful.

Step four: Use positive body language

✔ Stand tall, breathe deeply, and look people in the eye when you speak to them.

✔ Instead of anticipating the negative outcome, expect something positive.

✔ Listen actively to the other party and try putting yourself in their shoes so that you have a better chance of seeking the solution that works for you both.

✔ Inquire about their thoughts and feelings by using 'open' questions that allow them to give you a full response rather than just 'yes' or 'no'. Examples include: 'Tell me more about why . . . ', 'How do you see this working out? . . . ', and 'What are your thoughts on . . . ?'

✔ Don't let people talk down to you when you're sitting down. If they're standing, stand up too!

Step five: Recognise different communication styles

There are four types of communication style:

■ **passive/aggressive**—where you lose and do everything you can (without being too obvious) to make others lose too
■ **passive**—where you lose and everyone else wins
■ **aggressive**—where you win and everyone else loses
■ **assertive**—where everyone wins

It's important to appreciate that people communicate in a variety of ways. Your assertiveness therefore needs to be sensitive to a range of possible responses. Here are some tips on how to deal with the different communication styles outlined above:

✔ **Passive/aggressive people.** If you are dealing with someone behaving in a passive/aggressive manner, you can handle it by exposing what he or she is doing.

'I get the feeling you are not happy about this decision' or 'It appears you have something to say on this; would you like to share your views now?' In this way, they either have to deny their passive/aggressive stance or they have to disclose their motivations. Either way, you are left in the driving seat.

✔ **Passive people.** If you are dealing with a passive person, rather than let them be silent, encourage them to contribute so that they can't put the blame for their disquiet on someone else.

✔ **Aggressive people.** When confronting an aggressive communicator, try not to let the situation get out of hand. One option is to start by saying 'I'd like to think about it first': this gives you time to gather your thoughts and the other person time to calm down. When you're feeling put upon, it's important to remember that you have as much right as anyone to speak up and be heard.

Conflict is notorious for bringing out aggression in people. However, it is still possible to be assertive in this context. You may need to show that you are taking them seriously by reflecting their energy. To do this, you could raise your voice to match the volume of theirs, then bring the volume down as you start to explore what would lead to a win-win solution. 'I CAN SEE THAT YOU ARE UPSET and I would feel exactly the same if I were you . . . however . . . ' Then you can establish the desired outcome for both of you.

If you become more assertive, people won't necessarily think that you have become more aggressive. Be responsive to their communication styles, and their needs will be met too. All that will happen is that your communication style will become more effective.

TOP TIP
Once you become assertive, your confidence levels will be boosted, yet you need to have sufficient levels of confidence to try it in the first place. If you feel you lack the confidence to confront people, try the technique out in a safe environment first so that you get used to how it feels, then you can start to use it more widely.

Common mistakes

✗ **You go too far at first**
Many people, when trying out assertive behaviour for the first time, find that they go too far and become aggressive. Remember that you are looking for a win-win, not a you-win-and-they-lose situation. Take your time. Observe yourself in action. Practise and ask for feedback from trusted friends or colleagues.

✗ **Others react negatively to your assertiveness**
Your familiar circle of friends will be used to you the way you were, not the way you want to become. They may try

and make things difficult for you. With your new assertive behaviour, this won't be possible unless you choose it. If you find you're in this situation, try explaining what you're aiming to do and ask for their support. If they're not prepared to help you, you may wish to choose to let them go from your circle of friends.

STEPS TO SUCCESS

✔ Try to avoid feeling resentful—if you are feeling 'put upon', act on it!

✔ Remember that sometimes passivity is the best approach. Don't mistake aggressiveness for assertiveness!

✔ Speaking positively and using positive body language will encourage others to take you seriously and help you to feel you're taking control.

✔ It's important to listen carefully to other people's opinions so you are clear about which points you differ on, and which points you agree on.

✔ Try your techniques out in a safe environment until you feel comfortable with them.

✔ Build up a toolkit of assertive techniques and responses that have worked for you in the past and reuse them.

Words of wisdom

'I think I'm fairly naturally assertive – typical for the youngest in the family with two older brothers, probably. However, I've had to learn to manage this so that I'm effectively assertive. For example, when you think a discussion is not addressing the point in question, there is a right way of going about bringing everyone back in focus without being seen as bombastic.'

Stephanie Manuel
Stagecoach Theatre Arts plc

'In the early days, I wasn't always an extrovert but I've learned that shrinking violets don't get anywhere and I've had to work to get myself heard. If you always pitch yourself as a cottage industry, or as a one-woman band, then that's where you'll stay.'

Joy Nichols
Nichols Employment Agency

'As a child, I was painfully shy, I couldn't talk to people at all. When in business with my husband, I kept in the background - I always said 'I'd rather clean the loos than talk to the customers.' But when my husband died, I had to become assertive to survive. The first thing I did was to sign up for an assertive course and the key thing I learned was the big difference between assertiveness and aggression.'

Avril Owton
The Cloud Hotel

Developing presence

Presence is an elusive human quality that mysteriously enables someone to command respect, or at least attention. Individuals with presence seem to assert themselves effortlessly.

Some people believe you are born with presence; others, that it develops as a by-product of success. In fact, it is probably a combination of the two—and almost anyone can nurture and develop it.

Presence most often stems from confidence in what you're doing, when you feel most at home with, or passionate about, your role. Conversely, it's most likely to elude you when you feel uncomfortable or unsure of yourself.

Step one: Make yourself comfortable

It's important that you are physically comfortable with how you appear and how you feel. Here are the main areas to focus on when considering how to manage your body.

1 Health and fitness

✔ Look after your physical wellbeing through exercise, a good diet, proper rest, and relaxation techniques such as yoga or meditation.

2 Clothes

✔ Wear clothes you feel comfortable in and that fit well in order to help your posture and improve your confidence. They don't have to be expensive or conventional, just carefully chosen to suit the occasion.

3 Body language

✔ Look for opportunities to project a 'bigger' persona with your physical behaviour. By being aware of and controlling your mannerisms, movements, and demeanour, you are shaping the impact that your presence has on other people. See the box below for some key aspects of body language.

Body language points

✔ **Watch your posture**. Good posture is a great way of increasing your presence and stature. By standing and moving well, you project confidence and calm.
✔ **Maintain steady eye contact**. By making good eye contact with people, whether engaging with them individually or as an audience, you create an impression of honesty, confidence, and directness.

✔ **Demonstrate you are listening**. Paying attention to what people say and showing that you have heard their comments is important. So, too, is remembering people, and the context in which you know them. A useful tip for remembering someone's name is to repeat it when you are introduced, or to use it once or twice in conversation. An audience will pay more attention to you if they feel that you're paying attention to them in return.

✔ **Use appropriate gestures**. Fuller, sweeping arm gestures, rather than small hand movements or pointing fingers, will make a more positive impression. You don't want to overdo it, though, so try rehearsing in front of a mirror first.

It's a good idea to practise all these things, especially if you often feel nervous as a public speaker. A great way to begin would be to give a presentation on a subject that you feel passionate about.

TOP TIP
You can create an impression of being larger than you actually are by using the space around you. For example, when sitting, you might have one arm resting on the back of the chair, your body at an angle, and one leg crossed over the other. This position takes up a large amount of space and is very confident and imposing.

Step two: Prepare your mind

Your mind is one of the most important tools for creating presence. It can create a positive impression—on you as well as others—purely by imagining an idea. Here are some techniques you can use:

1 Visualisation

Our thoughts always precede our actions and behaviour so, by making an intention clear in your mind, you will already be influencing the way you create it in reality. This is the power of positive thinking.

✔ Try to visualise yourself as a person who emanates presence. For example, if you have to make a presentation, first picture the situation in your head and look at it in detail. Examine the feelings you get as you imagine the sound of an audience applauding, and the glow of achievement as you make your exit.

2 The 'anchor' technique

If, as many people find, you perform well in one situation but not in another, your mind can help here too.

✔ Think of a situation in which you feel comfortable or of some activity that you know you are really good at. Then link that feeling to a gesture, movement, or saying—such as pinching your thumb and forefinger together. This becomes the 'anchor', and when you repeat your anchor in a new setting, all the memories of performing well will flood back and help you to do so again.

TOP TIP

A common problem is to feel that the presence and credibility you have with some people, perhaps junior colleagues, disappears in front of others, for example, older people and peers. With junior colleagues, you have three things that they don't: knowledge, expertise, and authority. Your peers probably do have the same or more of these things—or they create the illusion that they do—and this can be sufficiently intimidating to make you lose your confidence. Try the 'anchor' technique to help you carry the confidence you feel with junior colleagues into situations with peers.

3 Positive affirmations

By telling yourself 'I am confident', 'I feel good', 'I have presence', you can subconsciously begin to influence your outward behaviour.

✔ Repeat your positive affirmations regularly so that they become the dominant messages you transmit about yourself.

TOP TIP
When repeating positive affirmations to yourself, make sure they are in the present tense. If you say, 'I *will* be confident', your brain will believe it to be a *future* scenario—and you may never get there!

Step three: Know what you know

It's important to acknowledge your areas of expertise. These are the topics that you feel you have mastered and that you're therefore most comfortable addressing. Remember that you have useful things to say and that people want to hear them.

✔ Use the knowledge and experience you have built up over the years to practise being confident in what you say and do. Make sure that people know your worth by being open and honest: share your experiences, tell stories, and engage people at a human level.

Bear in mind that you're not the only person who needs to have their presence acknowledged. People on a mission to assert their presence often stop seeing and listening to others.

✔ Try to be inclusive, and a reputation for 'generosity' will also become part of your presence.

Step four: Create the occasion

Projecting presence demands an occasion. This may be any type of event, from a one-to-one client meeting, to a gathering of a few people, or a formal presentation to a large audience. People with presence are able to create a sense of occasion in even the most ordinary of circumstances, such as walking along the production line, chairing a meeting, or giving a presentation.

✔ Think through your dramatic strategy, and practise so that you get the timing and pace right.

Projecting presence is a responsibility. Presence is about transmitting a quality that others trust and respond to. It makes them feel as if they are gaining something just from being close to you. For those who look up to you, you will be providing guidance and inspiring confidence, reflecting their values, and—perhaps—being their conscience.

✔ It's important that you are fully committed to your desire for presence, and not pursuing a power trip!

Common mistakes

✗ **You mistake over-confidence for presence**
As developing presence is closely linked to developing self-confidence, it's all too easy to overstep the line and come across as self-interested and over-confident.

Ironically, the very people who show over-confidence are often those most lacking in confidence, and they may be trying to compensate for this. But it's important to remember that part of developing presence is taking an interest in and building relationships with other people.

✗ You think presence cannot be developed
Some people are born with a certain amount of natural presence. Nevertheless, it's a gift that needs attention and development to mature properly. Look for occasions where you can practise the techniques that will help you project the impression you seek. In time, it will become second nature.

✗ You aren't fully prepared
Although there are four steps involved in creating presence, it's important to have an organic approach to them all. It's no use looking good, having a clear intention, and creating the occasion—but having nothing to say. Or conversely, imagine having a great story or piece of information, but getting the timing all wrong. Each element assists and supports the others, so you need to pay careful attention to them all.

STEPS TO SUCCESS

✔ Take care of your physical wellbeing.

✔ Dress comfortably and appropriately to the occasion.

✔ Build up physical confidence.

✔ Use the space around you to create a bigger persona.

✔ Visualise positive scenarios and how it feels to emanate presence.

✔ Use gestures or sayings as 'anchors' — transferable markers that you associate with doing something really well.

✔ Repeat positive affirmations about yourself.

✔ Be confident in the things that you know.

✔ Be aware of those around you.

✔ Create a sense of occasion.

Mastering all these elements will open new doors of opportunity for you: people will gravitate to you, offer you new leadership roles or new business, and spread the good word about your qualities and skills.

Words of wisdom

'When I've got a difficult meeting or a discussion where I know I've got to be on the ball, it all has to start when I get up. Being positive from the start. I always make a point of dressing with care, knowing that certain things will make me feel better about myself. It all gives you a good springboard.'

Stephanie Manuel
Stagecoach Theatre Arts plc

Building confidence at work

Confidence is a cornerstone of assertiveness. For those who are blessed with it, it's unremarkable. For those who do not have it, it's an extraordinarily difficult quality to develop and sustain.

We all have moments when our confidence blossoms—when we feel good about ourselves, have the knowledge we need to overcome any doubts, and are able to achieve any goal, however large or small. So we know what we are missing when confidence is lacking and, in the act of noticing its absence, we diminish the possibility of bringing it back to the surface.

Fear is the main emotion that undermines confidence. We can become flustered purely by the 'what if' scenarios that we conjure up in our minds. It is this irrational fear that needs to be addressed because, until it is dealt with, you won't have the confidence to assert yourself fully.

Step one: Know your job

Confidence cannot be put on like a coat—it has to be rooted firmly in the psyche. If you play-act at having confidence, it comes across as empty or brash. It may help you get through a situation, but it won't fuel the development of this quality in the longer term. Unfortunately, building confidence requires hard work.

Confidence comes from knowing what to do, how to do it, and when to do it. This know-how may be learned in a college or university setting, or it may have been developed on the job. Knowledge allows you to work within clear boundaries of competence. You will then become recognised for your abilities, reinforcing your self-image and building your confidence.

✔ If you are put into a different situation where you don't have the same level of familiarity, your confidence may be shaken. In this case, focus first on your transferable skills before developing the other abilities you will require.

TOP TIP
People often lose their confidence when they face obstacles to achieving their goals, and many are tempted to go back to their old comfort zone. If you are suffering this kind of anxiety, ask for feedback from others or consider coaching to enable you to expand your skills and build the confidence you need to succeed.

Step two: Establish clear objectives

Confidence often increases with success, and success can only be proven when a goal or objective has been reached. Clear objectives allow you to monitor your progress and adjust your focus in order to achieve your aims.

✔ Don't be afraid to ask for targets from your manager or set them for yourself. Without this level of clarity, you could be prevented from enjoying success because no one has defined success in that context. Without objectives—and therefore without successes—people's enthusiasm and level of energy diminish, along with their confidence.

✔ Make sure your targets are clearly defined so that your criteria for success are unambiguous. Poorly articulated objectives cause more personal grief in organisations than almost anything else. It's incredibly disconcerting to find that you are pouring energy into a professional void.

Step three: Unite authority and accountability

Nothing is more disheartening than taking the blame for something that is not your fault. Such knock-backs are damaging to confidence and motivation. Being accountable for failure without having the authority to make decisions can be extremely stressful.

✔ Talk to others in order to define the boundaries and responsibilities of your role. You may need to explain that this is not an attempt to avoid accountability, but rather an initiative to clarify your goals and thereby focus your efforts.

✔ Confidence comes from a job well done, so make sure that your stated objectives are dependent on your own performance, not that of others. If you are accountable for a project, you will take full credit for its success—and you will also be more motivated to make sure things run smoothly.

TOP TIP
Don't worry if you fall short of your targets at first. If you show improvement, your progress will be recognised. Always keep your results in perspective and take heart in your development.

Step four: Work on your personal development

Many organisations these days place responsibility for learning and development on the employee. However, it's worth reminding your employer that if you improve your skills, the company will benefit too. When a business invests in its people, it has a very positive effect on employees' confidence and their ability to contribute to the organisation's success.

✔ Enquire about your company's policy on training. It may even be mentioned in your employment contract. You might find that they offer assistance you weren't aware of. Organisational support is often given in the form of advice, mentoring, time off for study, or participation in special projects.

✔ Learning and development should be jointly planned and agreed upon by you and your organisation. This way, your new skills will be tailored to suit your job.

If you are self-employed, never neglect your own skills development, particularly those related to running your own business. As well as learning, the networking can be an inspirational boost.

TOP TIP
One of the essential ingredients of confidence is good communication. If you feel that you can communicate effectively in any situation—conveying thoughts to colleagues, building rapport with difficult clients, convincing journalists, and so on— your level of confidence will be high. It is therefore worth considering a course that will develop your communication skills.

Step five: Celebrate

Celebrations are very important. They are a way of acknowledging that an objective has been achieved and rewarding those responsible. They generate enthusiasm, build confidence, and boost morale.

A celebration can be as simple as a selection of cakes during coffee break; or it might be as elaborate as a large function to celebrate the achievement of organisational objectives or exceptional year-end results.

Although some people are internally driven—they don't need external recognition to make them feel as though they have succeeded—most people value some form of public appreciation.

✔ Make sure that you and your team celebrate your achievements. If necessary, remind others of the value of celebrations and persuade them to participate. If the successes are relatively small, you can still organise your own festivities.

✔ The prospect of a celebration can be a strong motivating factor. The thought of a bottle of champagne can be much more of an incentive than its cash value would suggest.

✔ The memory of a celebration will inspire confidence and enthusiasm in future projects.

TOP TIP
Public recognition not only validates your
contribution but also increases your visibility,
reinforcing your confidence and enhancing
your opportunities for promotion and
advancement.

Common mistakes

✗ **You fail to delegate**
Many managers feel the burden of accountability so
heavily that they no longer have the confidence to
delegate. They feel that allowing their people the
freedom to make decisions will result in a loss of control.
Due to this fear, they control the decision-making, and
alienate their team in the process. Keeping strict control
can actually disable the team and undermine the
confidence they have in their own abilities. This will
subsequently affect results and dent your own
confidence.

✗ **You become dependent**
If you are lucky enough to have a mentor or a supportive
partner, you can become dependent on their advice. This
is particularly common after promotion. You may well
have the skills to do the job, but after a while, you can
lose the confidence to make your own decisions.
Perhaps your mentor has contributed to this problem

by being too protective or not giving you enough freedom. You will have to wean yourself off their expertise. Raise this issue with them and identify areas or projects that you can begin managing without support.

✗ You fear the worst
Rather than concentrate on what you can control, you allow your mind to entertain thoughts of disaster. Confidence comes from doing what you do well, so focus on your core skills. Get the basics right and minor problems will not be significant. If you have clearly defined areas of accountability, you should be able to anticipate and overcome any worrying issues.

STEPS TO SUCCESS

✔ Know which skills you need to do your job. If you lack some of them, don't be afraid to ask for advice or training.

✔ Make sure you have clearly defined targets. Set yourself personal goals if necessary.

✔ Take control of your work. Ensure that you are not accountable for results over which you have no authority.

✔ Seek out opportunities for training. Confidence comes from knowledge and skills.

✔ Celebrate your achievements, to build confidence and raise your profile.

Words of wisdom

'You've got to make the time for yourself and your own self-development. I went to business school for a year. Not everyone in a small business can afford the time to do that. But whatever you need, you've got to expose yourself and take that step out of the business. Learning by doing and leading by example is key.'

Dawn Gibbins
Flowcrete Group plc

'Delegate as much as you can. Let people make their mark on a project and allow them to make mistakes – it's all part of their learning process, too.'

Liz Jackson
Great Guns Marketing

'Know your onions! You cannot bluff it. It's so difficult to get an appointment with people these days, so when you do, you have to know what you're doing. You can't leave anything to chance. Know your limitations, too. Problems start when you overstretch yourself and get out of your depth. In my employment agency, if I can't supply a brain surgeon, I have to be honest enough to say, 'Sorry, I don't do brain surgeons'.'

Joy Nichols
Nichols Employment Agency

'You need to know what you want out of a situation, to have clear goals. To be clear about what you're saying to people but still be pleasant.'

Avril Owton
The Cloud Hotel

Managing others' perceptions

We all hold differing views of the world, partly because of our different cultural backgrounds, life experiences, and personal values. Naturally, these influence the way we interact with one another. Our behaviours, competences, style, and approach further affect our relationships.

However, we are not entirely products of our past—we are consciously capable of modifying our conduct and, in turn, affecting the impression we make on others. Learning how to project a positive image of ourselves can be an invaluable tool in many areas of our lives, but especially in the workplace.

In senior management roles, it is particularly important to understand and manage the way we are regarded.

This is not as difficult as you might think. Although it requires a good deal of thought, motivation, and self-awareness, with practice you'll soon find it easier to assert your personality, motivate people, and lead them in a desired direction.

Step one: Overcome your misgivings

1 It's not about deception

Some people feel that changing the way you are perceived is a form of deception; they believe it involves pretending you are something you're not. However, managing perceptions is more about shedding light on your positive aspects while minimising the visibility of your weaknesses. It's not about deceit. It's about letting your true talents shine through.

2 It's a part of life

We live in a culture where people and organisations spend enormous sums of money hiring others to manage perceptions. The same skills used by advertising and public relations companies can be employed by you to influence those around you.

✔ Be aware of the impression your behaviour creates. This is the first step towards perception management. Gradually, you can develop skills that help you to manage your behaviour in a way that will move you forward in the direction you want.

3 It can help you in your career

In the modern employment market, there is a greater onus on autonomy. Careers are no longer managed by organisations, but are directed by individuals themselves. You are judged not only on what you do, but on how you do it — so evaluation by others now plays an important role in your development. People who can manage perceptions are likely to receive more offers and find fewer obstacles in their path.

TOP TIP

No matter in which capacity you meet people, take care of your relationships, because you never know when you might encounter the same people! People can harbour grudges for years, and you don't want to risk encountering an unforgiving individual in a position of influence. If you find it impossible to change your attitude, you'd better have skills that make you indispensable!

Step two: Understand how you are perceived

To understand how others view you, you must have an accurate understanding of yourself. Building self-awareness requires courage, commitment, and forgiveness.

✔ Firstly, encourage informal feedback from trusted peers. Remember that people will be giving you *their* opinions and these may not resonate with you—you may be surprised at the way you are perceived. Try to remain objective and find out where these views have come from.

✔ Use more formal tools that enable you to understand yourself, such as psychometric tests and personality profiles. The feedback from these is sometimes easier to manage because it's objective and has no third party involvement.

✔ Sometimes, 360-degree surveys are used to gather the views of different audiences, both inside and outside the business. These tend to focus on behaviour and competence. Be aware of the differences between the two. While both may be learned and modified, changing behaviour usually involves altering personality traits and perceptions and may be more difficult than acquiring new skills.

✔ When reviewing test results, try not to concentrate solely on personal information that is hurtful. Look for patterns in the feedback, and reflect on when and why these may have arisen. Pressure can often allow unintentional behaviour to come to the surface and this may have given rise to impressions that you would like to change.

TOP TIP

People generally hold onto first impressions, and it can be difficult to replace them with something more to your liking. Changing how others view you requires a consistent flow of new messages, and this means persistent awareness and self-evaluation—both of which take time and energy to develop.

Step three: Determine your strategy

Before embarking on any perception management strategy, establish what your goals are, how you are going to reach them, and how you will track your success.

✔ Don't be too ambitious at first: focus on one thing you can change that will create an immediate impression.

✔ Think of the context in which you are working, and use your feedback to select your initial goals.

Do

- Increase your own awareness.
- Be aware of your impact on others and interpret the signals they transmit to you.
- Be aware of the effect of pressure on you and how this looks to others.
- Be visible at strategic moments.
- Gently encourage feedback from people whose opinions you value.
- Allow others to have their choices.
- Give yourself time to change.
- Be consistent, patient, and forgiving of yourself and others.

Don't

- React emotionally to the feedback you receive.

- Get defensive.
- Become de-motivated.
- Become sycophantic.
- Get too big for your boots and try too hard too quickly.
- Expect too much.
- Embroil others in your views of yourself.
- Pester people for feedback.
- Be political or manipulative in your behaviour.

In a nutshell, perception management is all about creating an impression through conscious activities and awareness of your audience and the impact you have upon them. To succeed, you must:

✔ define your target audience

✔ be conscious of their values

✔ adjust your communication style

✔ encourage feedback

✔ be aware of how you adjust and adapt your behaviours

Step four: Gather support

While there may be encouragement to change your behaviour initially, remember that there may also be reactions to those changes. People are accustomed to the 'old' you and may have difficulty adjusting to the 'new' you. It is therefore important to do four things.

✔ Communicate your intentions to people who may be affected. If you have a formal annual performance appraisal, make it a 'learning objective', as this is likely to win more support and forgiveness if things don't work out quite the way you wish. You will also receive more praise when you are successful.

✔ Gain support from key members of your team to help keep you focused. A good support group is essential when seeking to change something about yourself. Extraordinary transformations have been achieved with the help of groups such as Alcoholics Anonymous and Weight Watchers.

✔ Find a coach to provide ongoing guidance. A coach will be able to offer impartial observations and encourage you to continue, or change, your strategy as you move forward. Coaching takes time and commitment, so you will need to allow for this in your work plan.

✔ Evaluate your progress at each milestone in your plan, either formally or informally. It is important to gather informal feedback regularly, but make sure you give people enough time to observe your new behaviour before asking for their opinions. You might warn those whom you are going to approach for feedback, so they can consciously pay attention to your behaviour. A more formal option is to revisit the 360-degree questionnaire and see whether others have noticed the change.

Don't lose heart if the changes in your approach are not immediately recognised by others. It may take months, so consistency and perseverance are essential.

TOP TIP
If you wish to change someone's impression of you, you must first understand both that person's existing perception and the one you wish to create. You then need to create a bridge between the two. Observe the person's values and behaviour and find an opportunity to convey a different message. However, you must be honest in the way you portray yourself. If you create an impression that is not essentially *you* the deception will be easy to spot, simply because living a lie is extraordinarily difficult to sustain.

Common mistakes

✗ You become impatient
It's easy to be impatient for results and give up too quickly. Behavioural change is not as easy as learning

a new skill; it requires dedication, commitment, and consistency. It is only through constant repetition and reinforcement of your new behaviour that people's perceptions will change.

✗ You don't ask for feedback

Some people are embarrassed to ask for feedback and help, particularly when they are in senior roles. This is because many forms of behaviour are habitual, and some may even have contributed to previous promotions. However, conduct appropriate to some roles may not be right for others. As your business grows and your role evolves, these differences are highlighted, when relationships suddenly become much more important than technical skills. In this situation, use a new project or a particular aspect of your role as a test-bed for the new you.

✗ You aim too high

In trying to change behaviours, people can be too ambitious and therefore lose the support of others. While it's important to be enthusiastic, try to understate rather than overstate your goals. It's always easier to deal with the surprise of your audience, rather than their disappointment.

STEPS TO SUCCESS

✔ Acknowledge the importance of perception management.

✔ Find out how people perceive you and how that differs from your own perception.

✔ Start small: begin by changing only one aspect of your image.

✔ Define your target audience, align your values with theirs, and adjust your communication style accordingly.

✔ Encourage feedback and involve other people in helping you sustain the change.

✔ Don't expect too much too soon.

Words of wisdom

'As a child, I was often described as a 'hothead' or a 'firebrand' and as an adult, I'm known as someone who speaks her mind. I know that this characteristic has had to be tempered by reason, kindness and compassion so that I'm effectively assertive and not seen as bossy or a bully.'
Stephanie Manuel
Stagecoach Theatre Arts plc

'When you enter what is traditionally a male domain, there is still an issue about women having to be formidable just to match men. For example, in a financial domain or in the political arena, I know I have to be assertive and have to work hard to convince male counterparts that I'm not a risk. But I always try not to compromise my personality. I suppose I've learned to use a bit of psychology. And if you do your homework, learn a bit about the person you're meeting, you'll quickly engage them in some way which makes you look confident and they have confidence in you.'

Joy Nichols

Nichols Employment Agency

Using non-verbal communication

Non-verbal communication involves many different 'channels' that convey meaning beyond what is being said. These include gestures, body movement, facial expressions, and even vocal tone and pitch. It's not an exact science, although we sometimes make judgments as if it were.

It's widely understood that the majority of information is conveyed through non-verbal signals, most of which come from the eyes. This explains why it's often hard to convey subtle meanings over the telephone or through the written word. Because the person receiving your message can't see your body or face, your meaning may well be misinterpreted.

If you can learn to employ non-verbal channels consciously, you will add a new dimension to your persuasive skills, enabling you to build rapport and assert your opinions to much greater effect. In addition, as part of the learning process, you will also develop skills that will enable you to read and interpret the non-verbal communication of others.

Step one: Match and mirror

If you watch two people talking in a relaxed and unself-conscious manner, you may notice that their bodies have taken on a similar demeanour. Both may have crossed their legs, or settled into their chairs in similar postures. If they are eating or drinking, they may do so at the same rate. This is called *matching* or *mirroring*, and it occurs naturally between two people who feel that they're on the same wavelength.

✔ Matching and mirroring can be used consciously as a technique to achieve rapport with someone, but you need to be subtle. Exaggerated mirroring looks like mimicry, and the other person is likely to feel embarrassed or angry.

TOP TIP

Even with a large audience, you can still build rapport. Suppose you are addressing a group of professionals from a podium. Make sure you seek information from everyone, acknowledge every contribution, give anyone who hesitates plenty of space, and support anyone who finds it difficult to speak in front of a group. If there are too many people in the room to pay attention to each one, invite contributions from those who are most extrovert and build rapport with them. This will give others confidence in your ability to connect with people.

✔ Observe what your counterparts do with their bodies as they're talking. Then follow the pattern of their non-verbal communication and reflect it back. Once this feels natural, try to take the lead by changing your body position and watch to see if they follow. You may well find that more often than not they do.

Once you begin to get a feel for this process, see if you can use it in a situation that is problematic. Perhaps there is someone at work with whom you do not have a good rapport. See if you can lead that person into a more relaxed exchange by practising the matching and mirroring technique.

TOP TIP

Sometimes, you might inadvertently convey the wrong message—perhaps you have a habit of using an expression or gesture that is commonly accepted to mean one thing when you really mean something different. A nervous laugh, for example, might indicate that you think you're being funny. You may, in fact, be trying to communicate something serious, but are nervous because the subject is a bit delicate. Training can help correct the most obvious quirks in your non-verbal lexicon. In the meantime it might help to acknowledge your idiosyncrasies publicly so people don't get the wrong impression.

Step two: Speak the same language

Neurolinguistic programming (NLP)

According to NLP (a method of tapping into the unconscious mind to reveal what is going on beneath the surface), language can indicate a great deal about how an individual views the world. Depending on which of the five senses they subconsciously favour, people may fall into one of five noticeable types:

- visual (sight)
- auditory (hearing)
- kinaesthetic (touch)
- olfactory (smell)
- gustatory (taste)

You can establish rapport with people more effectively by paying attention to their individual preferences for 'sensual' cues.

✔ When talking to someone you don't know well, listen to the kinds of words he or she uses. Once you have identified which of the five categories (see above) they belong to, respond by using the same kind of language. See the list on the next two pages for examples of some of the words to look out for.

In other words, when you are building rapport with someone, using the same kind of language is a subtle way of significantly enhancing the level of understanding between you.

Different types of vocabulary

Here are some examples of words and expressions that can help you identify the five different types of people:

- **visual language** includes terms like *see*, *appear*, *show*, *clear*, *picture*, *focused*, *well-defined*, *in light of*, *dim view*, *get a perspective on*, and *looks like*. For example, a person might say something like, 'I have a *vision* of what this organisation will *look* like in five year's time. I can *see* that it will take lots of energy to create what is in my *mind's eye*'. You can respond similarly: 'You build a very *clear picture* for me. I can *see* that this will be a challenge, but your *farsightedness* will surely enable you to reach your *dream*'.
- **auditory language** includes terms like *hear*, *listen*, *tune in/out*, *rumour*, *sound*, *clear as a bell*, *unheard of*, *word for word*, and *be all ears*. An auditory person might say, 'I *hear* that you have been promoted. You must have done a *resoundingly* good job!' You could respond, 'Yes, I have been *called* upon to *sound* out the market and *ring* some changes in the way we sell our products'.

44

- **kinaesthetic language** includes terms like *sense*, *feel*, *move towards*, *grasp*, *get hold of*, *solid*, *make contact*, *touch*, *concrete*, *pull some strings*, and *sensitive*.
- **olfactory language** includes terms like *smell*, *odour*, *rotten*, *aromatic*, and *fragrance*, and expressions like *turn your nose up* and *sniff out*.
- **gustatory language** includes terms like *bitter*, *sweet*, *sour*, *salty* and other taste-related words.

Step three: Listen actively

Active listening is a rare skill, but it is very effective in helping you build rapport with other people. It can also yield valuable information, enabling us to do our jobs more efficiently.

✔ Demonstrate that you have understood and are interested in what is being said in conversation. This kind of active listening requires good eye contact, lots of head nods, and responses such as 'Ah ha', 'Mmmm', and 'I understand what you mean'.

✔ Summarise what has been said to demonstrate your understanding, and ask open questions such as, 'Can you tell me more about . . . ?' and 'What do you think . . . ?'. These questions encourage further communication and enrich what is being communicated.

TOP TIP

People often try to cover up anger at work. However, their tone of voice, subtle changes in facial expression, and aggressive gestures are likely to convey their real emotions. For example, maybe someone will start pacing up and down or banging the table while still smiling pleasantly in an attempt to hide their true but socially unacceptable feelings. Active listening and open questions can help to defuse anger before it boils over.

Step four: Interpret in context

Much has been written about non-verbal communication, especially about how to read body language. This may give you insight into what is going on, but always remember to place your interpretation in context. For example, someone sitting in a meeting with his or her arms crossed is possibly being aggressive, reluctant, or disapproving. But, perhaps the person is shy, cold, or ill.

✔ Be cautious of jumping to conclusions about how someone is feeling without further information.

In a new environment with a different work culture, there could be a risk of misunderstandings at a non-verbal level. Some people are simply more emotional than others and expect a more energetic display of enthusiasm.

✔ Make sure you take time to observe what is going on around you and note how the different context makes you feel. When working with a new client, perhaps ask advice from someone in the culture who shares something of your own experience—they may be able to provide a useful communications bridge.

✔ In the first few weeks of working with someone new, beware of jumping to over-hasty conclusions based purely on non-verbal signals.

TOP TIP

Non-verbal messages can help you spot when someone is lying. Usually, when people are communicating in a straightforward way, their non-verbal signals are consistent with their words: they might say, 'I'm unhappy about that', and their face and body will droop too. When people are bluffing, their gestures are usually inconsistent with their speech. Someone may say, 'The deal is almost in the bag!'—but you notice a nervous body pattern, like the shifting of feet or the tapping of fingers. Unusual avoidance of eye contact or blinking can also indicate an inconsistency, which communication experts call *leakage*.

Common mistakes

X You lack subtlety

People new to the techniques of non-verbal communication can be over-enthusiastic practitioners. Observe yourself objectively to make sure you aren't offending others by broadly mimicking their speech or behaviour. Remember that most people instinctively send and interpret non-verbal signals all the time: don't assume you're the only one who's aware of non-verbal undercurrents. Finally, stay true to yourself. Be aware of your own natural style, and don't adopt behaviours that are incompatible with it.

X You ignore context

Putting too much store by someone's non-verbal signals can lead to misinterpretation and misunderstandings. It's important to understand the context in which the signals are being transmitted and think through the possible scenarios before jumping in.

X You over-emphasise non-verbal signals

Trying to control your meaning by emphasising your non-verbal signals can make you look ill at ease. It is very difficult to convey convincing messages that do not genuinely reflect what you think. Even if it is very subtle, leakage is bound to occur. This will raise people's suspicions and level of distrust. The best way to build rapport using non-verbal cues is to be authentic in what you say, and your body language will reinforce that message naturally.

STEPS TO SUCCESS

✔ Watch the body language of others and mirror it if you wish to build rapport. Use your own body language to influence tense situations and lead people into more relaxed exchanges.

✔ Observe the language used by those you wish to influence, listening out for 'sensual' cues. Enhance the level of understanding between you by tailoring your own choice of words to complement theirs.

✔ Listen attentively and actively: keep reassuring the other person that you're not just listening, but that you're interested in what he or she has to say.

✔ Think carefully before interpreting non-verbal signals, especially in a new and unfamiliar environment—there could be many reasons for unusual behaviour.

✔ Look out for leakage: non-verbal signals that either contradict or don't match what the person is saying. It can help you identify when someone is hiding something.

✔ Remember that other people know about these techniques and will be able to spot any obvious attempts to influence their opinions. Be subtle!

Words of wisdom

'Women in business have to stop being afraid. They seem afraid of their own shadow sometimes and they cocoon themselves away. You've got to be confident in your business and you've got to be passionate – that way, you can face the worst ogre.'

Joy Nichols
Nichols Employment Agency

'My assertiveness has really come from experience. I also get a great deal of inspiration from books. I once read 'Secrets' by Joan Collins, who herself claims to be quite shy deep down. She says when walking into a room of people, look your best, take a deep breath, throw your shoulders back and hold your head high. Your confidence really comes from inside you – knowing your business and knowing what you want and what you're trying to achieve.'

Avril Owton
The Cloud Hotel

'Body language is particularly important. How you present yourself. Finding time to have your hair and make up done before a presentation, even have a manicure. They can all help to relax me and make me feel calmer and more comfortable with myself. Deep breathing, tucking your tummy in and your shoulders back will make you look more confident.'

Christina Vaughan
Image Source

Dealing with stressful relationships and bullying

It can be very hard to assert yourself in the workplace if you have a difficult relationship with a more dominant colleague—or even a challenging client. It can be tempting to lay the blame for this type of situation at the other person's feet, due to his or her unreasonable, negative, awkward, or unhelpful behaviour. Whether justified or not, the good news is that there is plenty that you can do to change the dynamic of the relationship.

Abusive behaviour ranges from the extreme, such as bullying and physical abuse, to more subtle forms of harassment that are often more common but less recognised. What is tolerated in the workplace will depend very much upon the culture of the organisation and the attitudes of its leaders. Some businesses ignore all forms of harassment; others make a point of creating a culture where intimidation of any sort is cause for reprimand or dismissal.

It is worth reflecting on your organisation's culture to see what maltreatment exists, both on and under the surface.

Step one: Understand the forms bullying can take

The recipient of bullying is often in a weaker position, physically, emotionally, or hierarchically. Victims are usually unable or unwilling to stand up for themselves, due to what they feel will be the unacceptable consequences, such as an escalation of abusive behaviour or the threat of redundancy. This fear allows the behaviour to continue.

Any form of harassment can have a serious impact on the morale of staff in the business, and can affect the performance and health of individuals. Not only is it damaging, but it's also unlawful, and should be treated seriously.

Different forms of harassment

These include:

- all manner of physical contact from touching, pushing, and shoving, to serious assault
- intrusive or obsessive behaviour, such as constant pestering, baiting, or dogging a person's movements
- tricks being played that result in risk or danger to the individual
- group bullying, where the individual is overpowered by a number of aggressors

Less direct forms of harassment include:

- the spreading of rumours about the individual, making jokes or offensive personal remarks
- written statements, letters, or graffiti
- actions that isolate the individual and prevent them from doing their work effectively
- non co-operation, or sabotage of professional objectives
- pressure for sexual favours
- obscene gestures and comments
- the orchestration of situations that compromise the individual
- manipulative 'political' behaviours, that may include bribery or blackmail

TOP TIP

The difference between a good joke and bullying can be subtle. However, if the person being bullied is demeaned and disempowered in some way, or if the joke becomes personally critical and destructive, then the line has been crossed. It's important to remember that it's not the intention of the person playing the joke that determines whether the line has been crossed, it's the feelings it provokes in the victim.

Step two: Recognise the mental and physical impact

Don't be tempted to live with the difficulties of having a troublesome work colleague, or seek ways to minimise the impact he or she has on your working life. Avoidance tactics can be more time-consuming and stressful than being assertive and confronting the problem.

✔ Focus on your own health as this may encourage you to tackle the issue rationally and try to reach an accommodation that will prevent you from jeopardising your health or feeling that you have to leave your job.

Step three: Determine when the line has been crossed

Often, people find it hard to know whether the line of harassment has been crossed. If they confront the perpetrators, they can be accused of 'being a poor sport', or worse. Such accusations are often levelled to mask what is going on, and can seriously undermine the victim's confidence.

✔ Seek feedback from those who may have observed any incidents. Their account may give you more ammunition to deal with the problem appropriately. Select your witness carefully though—ones you can trust to be allies throughout the ordeal, who won't 'flip' on you under pressure.

Determining whether the harassment is trivial or serious is paramount. If it is infrequent and seems harmless, try not to take it too personally. Remember that bullying says more about the character of the bully than it does about the victim. However, if the bullying is persistent or escalates, you must confront it and report it. Even if you don't wish to face the bully head on, there are likely to be other ways of asserting yourself.

TOP TIP

If you suspect a case of bullying, but the perpetrator disguises his or her actions with jokes, one way of dealing with this is to write down the incidents in a journal, including the context in which they took place. Ask for feedback from observers and include their comments. Over time, you will be able to see if there is a pattern to the behaviour. Also, the record may be useful if you decide to take the matter further.

✔ There are probably procedures in place to assist you in dealing with your situation in the workplace. You may be advised to report the incident(s) but, should you feel uncomfortable about this, you may wish to go to the human resources department if you have one, or seek specialist external advice.

✔ If you decide to lodge a formal complaint, make sure you have a record of the incidents and a note of the witnesses present.

Step four: Deal with a difficult person

Many people have a challenging relationship to deal with at some point in their working life. When examining such a relationship, it's important to realise how much of it is due to the structure or culture of the organisation and how much is due to truly unreasonable behaviour. Looking at the wider issues in the organisation may provide the key to the problem. Acting upon your discoveries will require a combination of assertiveness and sensitivity.

| Understand the other person

A difficult relationship may simply be a personality clash. But it's rare that someone is consciously trying to be difficult.

✔ However uncomfortable it may feel, try putting yourself in the other person's shoes. Recognise the objectives that define his or her role and think through the pressures they are under. Make a mental list of their strengths, preferred working style, idiosyncrasies, values, and beliefs.

This will help you deepen your understanding. Very often, when we feel disliked or when we dislike someone, we avoid building this understanding and instead look for ways of avoiding the issues. But in the world of business, if we try to understand another's viewpoint, we can also learn so much about our own ability to work with people.

TOP TIP

If one individual is making work intolerable because of his or her moody and bad-tempered behaviour, try to work out how you could influence the situation for the better. Observe his or her behaviour to see if there is a pattern in it, and then try giving constructive feedback, letting them know how his or her mood swings affect you and the team. Use assertive language and ask if there is anything you can do to alleviate the cause of the problem.

2 Clarify objectives

Sometimes we just need to open up paths of communication in a busy office to ensure that difficulties are 'aired' and discussed. If you feel you're being challenged all the time by one individual, perhaps they don't understand fully what you're trying to achieve. If these objectives were shared and they were allowed to feel more a part of the team, their 'inflexibility' might disappear.

TOP TIP
**A lack of communication often contributes
to workplace misunderstandings. But
time your response to the individual
concerned with care. Approach them
when they are not under excessive stress –
we all feel less accommodating
and accepting under stress.**

3 Understand yourself

Sometimes, a lack of self-knowledge may lead to us being surprised by the feedback we get and our reactions to it. In getting to know yourself better, you may wish to ask for input from your colleagues.

✔ Ask your colleagues what they observe when you interact with others, how you come across to them, and how you could manage your communication differently. Although their perception may not represent the absolute truth about you, it nonetheless reflects the image you create.

4 Consider changing aspects of your behaviour

This often prompts a reciprocal behavioural change in the other person. If you don't change anything about the way you interact with them, the relationship will retain the same dynamics and remain unaltered, so this is definitely worth a try.

✔ Think through some of the past encounters you have had with this individual and reflect upon them objectively, perhaps with a friend or colleague who knows you well.

✔ Identify any recurring patterns in your interactions. Perhaps this situation happens over and over again, which suggests that you harbour a value or belief that is being repeatedly compromised. If you can understand what this is, you can learn to manage these situations more effectively.

Perhaps you value attention to detail, but the other person is a big-picture person. Every time you ask for more detailed information, you will be drawing attention to one of their vulnerabilities, and he or she is likely to become unco-operative or irritated by your request.

Once you have observed your respective patterns, you can work around them or accommodate them dispassionately.

5 Remember that a relationship is mutual

In order to be considered effective, managers need a co-operative and productive team. But in order to be part of such a team, each member needs their manager to provide the resources and support they need to do their job properly.

It's well known that some of the most stressful situations arise when dependents' needs are not met or their objectives are not clear. People find a variety of ways to deal with this. Some become angry and resentful of another's authority; some find ways of challenging decisions in order to assert some of their own power; and others become compliant saboteurs. It's rare in business to find relationships where there is absolutely *no* reciprocal power.

6 When all else fails . . .

Think carefully about whether you have the time and energy to tackle a difficult relationship. Your own health and self esteem matters, too. In some instances, you may have the ultimate power: to walk away.

TOP TIP

If it is your boss who is making you feel miserable by constantly making negative and derisive comments about the way you do your work, you need to find a private moment when you can explain how this makes you feel and ask your boss to stop doing it. You could suggest that he or she gives you clear guidelines and constructive feedback that will help you to meet his or her expectations and develop your talents. Point out that constant nagging affects the way you work and that you would be much more effective if he or she took a positive interest in what you do.

Common mistakes

✗ You mistake a genuine extrovert for a bully
Extroverts frequently speak their minds before really
thinking about what they are saying—which can
sound confrontational and be mistaken for harassment.
Being extroverts, however, they are often receptive
to questioning and keen to point out that they were
just testing the boundaries, or joking. By sharing
your perception and inviting theirs, it's possible
to clarify and dispel the situation without further
entanglement.

✗ You take 'difficult' behaviour personally
It is very tempting to take the behaviour of a difficult
person personally. However, it is very unlikely that *you*
are the problem. It may be something you do, it may be
the values you hold, or it may be that you remind that
person of someone he or she doesn't get on with.

✗ You don't remain detached
Many difficult relationships deteriorate to the point where
they are fraught with contempt and confrontation. This is
never helpful in a work setting and only makes matters
uncomfortable for everyone. If you find yourself being
drawn into an angry exchange, try to remain emotionally
detached and listen actively to what is being said (or
shouted) to you. It may provide you with clues about
why the situation has developed and allow you to get
straight to the point of concern. Ask for a private

review afterwards to explore the incident. This may bring to the surface issues that are relatively easy to deal with and that will prevent further outbursts from occurring.

✗ **You never confront the issue**
Because facing up to harassment is so difficult, many people avoid biting the bullet. Inactivity will only prolong a miserable situation. Acquiescence enables bullying to thrive and allows the aggressors to maintain the power imbalance. Try taking responsibility for your share of the problem and examine what it is you may be doing to provoke conflict between you and your colleague.

STEPS TO SUCCESS

✔ Be aware that there are many kinds of bullying, most of which do not involve physical abuse. You may be suffering in more ways than you know.

✔ Realise that inactivity is not an option. The only thing you're likely to achieve by doing nothing is endangering your self esteem and jeopardising your health.

✔ Ask others for their opinions on whether what you witness constitutes bullying.

✔ If the line has been crossed, resolve to take action. Select your witnesses carefully and keep a record of the bullying incidences.

✔ Your first step should be to go through formal, established channels rather than confronting the issue on your own.

✔ If your relationship with your boss is problematic, try to see it from both sides and understand why he or she may act the way they do.

✔ You may be able to improve the relationship a great deal by slightly modifying your own behaviour.

✔ If all else fails, you can always retain your power and walk away.

Words of wisdom

'When I'm faced with a difficult situation – perhaps a relationship at work that simply isn't working – it can make me very low. And dealing with it is never comfortable. But I always try and build a bridge in my mind to the blue skies beyond and bear in mind that what I'm doing now will help bring a better future.'

Stephanie Manuel
Stagecoach Theatre Arts plc

'When you've got a problem to resolve, talking to a member of staff about a difficult issue or making a tricky phone call for example, always do it first thing in the morning. It's not usually as bad as you think it will be, it doesn't prey on your mind for the rest of the day, and after that, nothing else will feel worse! Shouting never does any good, of course. Stick to your word and keep calm. After that, you can go home and have a good cry!'

Avril Owton
The Cloud Hotel

Improving leadership skills

There are many myths about leaders—'leaders are born and not made' being a prime example. The truth is that leadership depends on a combination of elements.

The personal qualities of the leader are indeed vital, as are the needs of those being led and the context in which they operate. Although there is no doubt that some personality types thrive better in leadership roles than others, the good news is that leadership skills *can* be learned. In the same way that you can work on your delegation skills and team management techniques, so you can develop the personal qualities you need to be a good leader, like assertiveness and self-confidence. Moreover, leadership is never a finished product; it's an ongoing process that needs continuous nurturing and refinement.

A lack of assertiveness can hold many people back from developing their true potential, particularly in the role of leader. It is one of the keys to successful leadership, together with sensitivity, and a thorough knowledge of the available approaches.

Step one: Understand leadership styles

There are many different styles of leadership. For example, think of three shepherds. The first opens the gate and walks through, allowing the flock to follow—this shepherd *leads from the front*. Another stands behind the sheep and pushes or guides them through, demonstrating a *supportive leadership style*. The third moves from front to back and sometimes to the middle of the flock, demonstrating an *interactive leadership style*.

✔ Learn how to apply different leadership styles as this can help you respond effectively in different situations. For leaders to exist, there must be followers, and the needs of followers change depending on the situation.

Another school of thought recognises four leadership styles: directive, process, creative, and facilitative. Each is related to a personality trait (see diagram below). So, being more

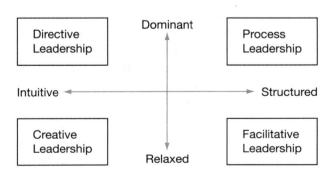

relaxed doesn't mean you can't be a leader. You simply have a natural inclination towards a certain type of leadership.

Evidently, certain styles are suited to particular situations. A structured leader is likely to succeed in a situation where process is important, for example, in running an operation. The relaxed or facilitative leader may be one who manages a professional group of people. Dominant leaders may be needed in organisations where there is a real drive for change. Usually a person with a strongly intuitive style of leadership can cope with most situations short-term.

✔ You may be able to learn other management styles— more dominant, intuitive, or structured—as you become more confident and practised in leadership. Try to work with your preferred style until you are comfortable enough to branch out.

TOP TIP
If your leadership skills have been called into question and the people you supervise seem unmotivated or unproductive, you or your team may be expected to display more commitment. The key to making this change is to think less about what you're doing, and spend more time planning how you do it. Think about how you are perceived—and whether their perceptions are accurate.

Step two: Learn leadership theory

Business leaders need to understand the guiding principles of their own organisation. Leadership programmes, frequently offered by business schools, provide the foundation of such understanding.

✔ Choose the right course for you. Topics range from business theory to strategic planning to understanding risk. They might also cover organisational behaviour, which analyses what makes people tick (and, therefore, how to manage them), and marketing. You might also find classes on marketplace analysis, encompassing competitor evaluation.

Having well-developed commercial awareness and a good business education will not only give you confidence, but will also help you command respect from others.

TOP TIP
Once you have learned the theory of
leadership, you'll need to find an opportunity
to put it into practice. You may be taking on
a new team or building one up from scratch.
It may be helpful to have a mentor to
support you in these early stages.

Step three: Build self-awareness

Your leadership style is the means by which you communicate with the rest of the organisation. The more self-aware you become, the more effectively it will work for you.

Areas of self-awareness

Self-awareness means understanding and knowing:

- what you are like
- what your preferences are
- what your goals are
- how other people perceive you and your goals
- how you are motivated to achieve them

✔ Try out some of the numerous tests and questionnaires designed to help you explore your personality and preferences. These are widely available from books, the Internet, consultancies, and other sources.

✔ Surveys can also be useful. Most business schools have valuable data on expected leadership behaviours.

✔ Once you've completed this consultation process, combine the information from all these sources to establish a benchmark for yourself.

Step four: Learn from other people's experience

It is often said that 'knowledge is power'. Certainly, a superior level of knowledge will give you an advantage over your peers, making you more suited to leadership positions. Therefore, you should always look for opportunities to learn from others' expertise. Some of the most obvious opportunities you should take advantage of if you can are:

✔ **Coaching.** This is useful in situations where there are behavioural, skills, or confidence gaps.

✔ **Training programmes.** Whether developed within or outside your organisation, training can give you an insight into your abilities as well as expanding them.

✔ **Networking.** Talking to leaders you admire or simply sharing your experiences with others can help you gain a greater awareness of the traits required for leadership.

Step five: Broaden your own experience

In the medium term, there are a number of other strategies ycu can employ to increase your knowledge, your confidence, and your ability to lead.

✔ **'Stretch' assignments.** These are tasks that extend your horizons but have no negative consequences for your present job should you fail. They are particularly good for people who like to learn on the job.

✔ **Lateral transfers.** You can develop leadership skills more comprehensively by working in different parts of the organisation. This will help you gain a better understanding of how the company works (and why) and provides a useful opportunity for you to work with people outside your 'comfort zone'.

✔ **Benchmarking against peers in other companies.** By gathering information and advice from people who work for different organisations, you can benefit from each other's experience and measure your progress.

✔ **Working outside your comfort zone.** You cannot learn if you always stick within the boundaries of what you know. Take on a project that scares you, challenges you, and offers new experience.

TOP TIP
Many people have trouble transferring leadership skills from outside the workplace into the office environment. Perhaps the outside leadership role is voluntary, or came about because of a passion for that particular project or leisure activity. If so, look at

---

**what allows you to thrive in your external
leadership role. Understanding such factors
as your motivation and the support you
receive may help you to see what is missing
at work. Then you can move towards
creating the right context there too.**

Step six: Apply your leadership skills

Leadership opportunities are often thrust upon us
unexpectedly. However, if you have followed the above
steps and prepared yourself properly, you will be in a
strong position to make the most of the change. Here
are a few practical tips to help you get off to a good
start.

✔ In most cases, your best bet is to begin with an analysis
of the situation. Decide what is needed, and how you
can best achieve it.

✔ Some leadership positions require you to set the
objectives for others to follow. In these situations,
scheduling, consultation, and team building are essential
to success.

✔ Leaders often need to work as intermediaries between
two groups—those wanting the results (boards or
executive groups, for example), and those who will
deliver the results. In this case you need to establish
good communication channels with both parties.

✔ Try to pick teams that have a good balance between competent managers and energetic, loyal team members. Teams need consistent, positive energy levels to sustain momentum. Therefore, choosing a team according to the mix of talent required, rather than based on friendships or politics, is critical.

✔ If you are trying out new systems or approaches, surround yourself with the right people, create a framework for support, and document the process so you can later evaluate what you have done.

TOP TIP
Leadership capability does not emerge overnight; it takes time and practice. Part of the process involves learning about yourself and your responses to situations that call for leadership. Use this knowledge to assess what has worked and what hasn't, in order to plan your approach next time.

Common mistakes

✗ **You don't realise the changes that a leadership role entails**
People often try to retain the relationships they enjoyed before taking on a leadership position. Leaders, especially those in supervisory roles, must be careful not to let friendships interfere with good judgment.

Be aware, too, that those who know you as a colleague or peer may have a different view of you as a leader.

✗ You mirror other leaders too closely

People new to leadership roles may try to copy a leader they respect, because the person provides an easy model. This can create a false impression of what you are really like, or, worse, make you look foolish for trying to mimic a style incompatible with your own personality. Leadership behaviours come from within. Understand what it is you respect in the other leader and think about how you can best display that attribute. If it doesn't work, don't be afraid to try a new approach.

✗ You don't work at it

Many people hope that they have natural leadership skills, and accept leadership positions without proper training or mental adjustment. This sink-or-swim approach works sometimes, but not always!
Building up leadership skills, increasing awareness of yourself, and developing a positive reputation in the organisation have much more potential for success. It will also give you more room to make mistakes without losing credibility.

✗ You mistake public speaking for leadership

Commanding an audience is a great skill, and many leaders have it. However, it is not the sole requirement. Leaders also need to be problem-solvers and have originality, flair, confidence, self-knowledge, strong interpersonal skills, the ability to listen, vision, good organisational skills, and so on. The ability to 'talk a good fight' is not enough on its own.

STEPS TO SUCCESS

✔ Recognise that leadership is a skill that we can all acquire, rather than a natural talent reserved for a privileged few.

✔ Identify different leadership styles and establish when each one might be appropriate.

✔ Find your own natural style of leadership before developing others.

✔ Learn as much as you can from all the available resources: courses, textbooks, websites, and more experienced peers or mentors.

✔ Look for opportunities to acquire and practise your leadership abilities. Be brave enough to venture into new territory, expanding your experience, building confidence, and developing new skills.

✔ When presented with a leadership opportunity take time to analyse the situation, set clear objectives, and pick a good team that is competent, loyal, and energetic.

Words of wisdom

'It took me some time to realise the bit about leading by example. But now I can see how important it is. I allow all the team time off and pay for them to go on a volunteer project and I volunteer myself too. That's a cost to bear but once people live it and do it, they're then the best sales people we have in our business.'

Deirdre Bounds
i-to-i.com

'Understanding the people, getting the people to buy into the values and culture my father and I had was the most difficult thing for me. As a new business, and knowing each other so well, there wasn't any consistency in what we did. I know now as a leader, you've got to see the future, be the visionary and share the vision. Getting everyone to buy into where the business is going.'

Dawn Gibbins
Flowcrete Group plc

'You have to become a multi-tasking leader: innovatory, motivational, visionary. You've got to adapt to a different style of leadership depending on who you're dealing with. Individuals are all very different and have different needs. There's no one-size-fits all leadership style.'

Perween Warsi
S & A Foods Ltd

Where to find more help

Our recommended reads for this topic also include the following books and can be purchased online at the **everywoman** bookshop. Go to www.everywoman.co.uk/bookshop

---

Agreed: Improve Your Powers of Influence
Terry Gillen
London: Institute of Personnel and Development, 1999
174pp ISBN: 0852928017
The author describes techniques for increasing the influence that we, as individuals, exert, and for achieving the outcomes that we, as individuals, desire. He explores each of the key principles involved: persuading, probing, listening, assertiveness, understanding behaviours, interpreting body language, giving constructive criticism, and resolving differences of opinion.

Assertiveness
Terry Gillen
London: Institute of Personnel and Development, 1998
96pp ISBN: 085292769X
The author explores the nature of assertiveness and examines its effects on our working lives. Focusing on self-assessment and evaluation, he discusses the process of thinking and behaving assertively and puts forward a plan to develop more assertiveness in the reader's own behaviour.

Assertiveness at Work: A Practical Guide to Handling Awkward Situations
Ken Back, Kate Back
New York: McGraw-Hill Education, 1999
224pp ISBN: 0077095332
Aimed at managers, this popular guide offers advice on developing an assertive approach at work while minimising conflict. It includes exercises to aid learning and new chapters on negotiating, dealing with bosses, and assertiveness during times of change.

The Assertiveness Workbook
Randy J. Paterson
Oakland, California: New Harbinger Publications, 2000
200pp ISBN: 1572242094
This book encourages us to express our ideas and stand up for ourselves, both at work and in our personal relationships. Step-by-step guidance uses cognitive-behavioural techniques to improve communication skills, and case studies show how these skills have been used successfully.

Body Language at Work
Adrian Furnham
London: Institute of Personnel and Development, 1999
82pp Management Shapers Series ISBN: 0852927711
This book offers an introduction to the significance of body language and what it reveals about attitudes and emotions. It also presents techniques for interpreting nonverbal gestures and expressions and considers how they might be used in work situations.

Personal Power
Philippa Davies
London: Piatkus Books, 1996
192pp ISBN: 0749916427
Using case histories and role models, the author sets out strategies for developing confidence and charisma, thereby becoming more assertive and successful. Guidance is also given for building up influence and developing the skills of persuasion and negotiation.

When I Say No, I Feel Guilty
Manuel J. Smith
New York: Bantam, 1985
352pp ISBN 0553263900
This best-selling book offers a range of strategies to help people feel comfortable asserting their needs at work and at home. It also offers advice on how to combat manipulation and emotional game-playing by other people.